GOODNIGHT STORIES FOR KIDS

INTEGRITY   RESPECT   KINDNESS   VALUES

Copyright

©2024 HANI FAWAREH

Preface

Welcome to the second installment of "Islamic Stories For Kids: Prophet Muhammad and the Companions." In this collection, we continue our journey into the lives of the noble Prophet Muhammad (peace be upon him) and his esteemed Companions, presenting 30 captivating tales of virtue and wisdom. As with the first book in the series, our aim is to provide young readers with meaningful narratives that not only entertain but also impart valuable lessons and moral insights rooted in Islamic teachings.

Prophet Muhammad (peace be upon him) remains a timeless source of inspiration, and the Companions, who stood by his side through triumphs and challenges, exemplify the highest standards of character and devotion. Through these stories, children will not only learn about the historical events that shaped early Islam but also gain a deeper understanding of the virtues, values, and principles that continue to guide the Muslim community.

Each tale is crafted to engage young minds, fostering an appreciation for the rich cultural and spiritual heritage of Islam. The stories highlight qualities such as compassion, courage, honesty, and perseverance, encouraging children to reflect on their own actions and aspire to embody these virtues in their daily lives.

As parents, educators, and caregivers, we play a crucial role in nurturing the next generation. This book serves as a tool to facilitate meaningful conversations about faith, morality, and the importance of character development. By sharing these stories with our children, we contribute to their moral and spiritual growth, helping them navigate life with the wisdom and grace exemplified by Prophet Muhammad (peace be upon him) and his Companions.

May this collection of tales be a source of joy, inspiration, and guidance for young readers, fostering a love for the beautiful teachings of Islam. As we embark on this literary journey, let us strive to pass on the timeless wisdom encapsulated in these stories, creating a lasting impact on the hearts and minds of our beloved children.

May the lessons learned from the lives of Prophet Muhammad and his Companions illuminate the path to virtue, shaping the character of the next generation with love, compassion, and a steadfast commitment to the principles of Islam.

Sincerely,

HANI FAWAREH

Table of Content

1. The Luminous Path: Prophet Muhammad's (PBUH) Journey of Mercy

Once upon a time, in the city of Mecca, a child was born to Amina bint Wahb and Abdullah ibn Abd al-Muttalib.

Little did the world know that this infant, named Muhammad, would grow up to become the last and final prophet of Islam, a beacon of mercy and guidance for humanity.

Muhammad's early life was marked by the loss of his father before his birth and his mother when he was just six years old. Orphaned, he found solace in the care of his grandfather, Abd al-Muttalib, and later, his uncle, Abu Talib.

As a young man, Muhammad earned a reputation for his honesty, integrity, and reliability. His wisdom caught the eye of Khadijah bint Khuwaylid, a successful businesswoman, who later became his wife. Their union was one of mutual respect, love, and partnership.

At the age of 40, Muhammad received his first revelation from the angel Gabriel while meditating in the Cave of Hira. Terrified and awestruck, he heard the words of Allah, beginning a series of revelations that would eventually form the Quran, the holy book of Islam.

Muhammad's mission was clear – to call people to the worship of the One God, to establish justice, and to show compassion to all of creation. Despite facing persecution and opposition, he continued to spread the message of Islam, gaining followers who would later be known as the Sahabah (companions).

The Hijra, the migration from Mecca to Medina in 622 CE, marked a pivotal moment. It symbolized a new beginning, a community built on justice, equality, and brotherhood.

Muhammad's leadership transformed the early Muslim community into a model of compassion and unity.

The Battle of Badr and the Treaty of Hudaybiyyah demonstrated not only the strength of the Muslims but also the Prophet's commitment to peaceful resolution whenever possible. His mercy extended even to his staunchest enemies.

The Farewell Sermon, delivered during the Prophet's final pilgrimage, encapsulated the essence of his teachings. He emphasized the equality of all believers, the sanctity of life and property, and the importance of brotherhood among Muslims.

Prophet Muhammad's life serves as a timeless example of compassion, humility, and devotion to God. His legacy lives on through the Quran and the Sunnah, providing a guiding light for millions around the world. The story of Prophet Muhammad (PBUH) is a tale of mercy, resilience, and the transformative power of faith, inspiring generations to come.

2. Khadijah bint Khuwaylid: The Heart of Mecca

Once upon a time, in the bustling city of Mecca, there lived a remarkable woman named Khadijah bint Khuwaylid.

Her story, often overshadowed by the events that followed, is a testament to resilience, intelligence, and unwavering faith.

Khadijah was no ordinary woman. Widowed twice, she managed a successful caravan trade business with astuteness and integrity. Her reputation for honesty and fairness echoed through the marketplaces, earning her the title "Al-Sadiqah" (the truthful) and "Al-Aminah" (the trustworthy).

As fate would have it, news of Khadijah's business acumen reached the noble and respected merchant, Muhammad ibn Abdullah. Intrigued by her qualities, he sought her assistance in managing one of his trade caravans. Little did they know that this encounter would change the course of their lives forever.

Working closely together, Muhammad and Khadijah developed a deep bond founded on trust, respect, and shared values. As the caravan journeys unfolded, admiration turned into a profound connection, leading to a union that transcended the boundaries of business.

Khadijah, fifteen years Muhammad's senior, recognized in him qualities that set him apart from the rest—a rare honesty, compassion, and a profound spirituality. Despite societal norms, she proposed marriage to Muhammad, initiating a union that would become one of the most cherished in Islamic history.

Their marriage was not only a union of hearts but also a partnership in every sense. Khadijah stood by Muhammad during times of revelation, offering solace, support, and unwavering belief in the divine message he carried. She became the first person to accept Islam and remained a steadfast companion throughout the early challenges faced by the nascent Muslim community.

Khadijah's influence extended far beyond the domestic sphere. Her wisdom and generosity left an indelible mark on the hearts of those around her. Her commitment to social justice and care for the less fortunate became a cornerstone of her legacy.

Tragically, Khadijah's life was not without hardship. She bore the brunt of the economic sanctions imposed on the Muslim community in Mecca and suffered the loss of loved ones. However, her steadfast faith and resilience remained unwavering.

"Khadijah bint Khuwaylid: The Heart of Mecca" is a tale of a woman who, against the backdrop of a challenging and changing society, exemplified the virtues of strength, compassion, and unyielding faith. Her story serves as a beacon of inspiration, reminding us that true greatness lies in the service of others and the steadfast pursuit of righteousness.

3. Abu Bakr al-Siddiq: The Faithful Companion

Once upon a time, in the vibrant city of Mecca, there lived a man of impeccable character and unwavering faith named Abu Bakr al-Siddiq.

This is the story of his remarkable journey and steadfast commitment to Islam.

Abu Bakr was not just a close friend of Prophet Muhammad (PBUH) but his most trusted companion. In the early days of Islam, when the message of monotheism was met with skepticism and hostility, Abu Bakr stood firmly by the side of the Prophet, embracing the newfound faith with an open heart and unshakable conviction.

The story begins with Abu Bakr's conversion to Islam. Known for his honesty, integrity, and compassionate nature, he earned the title "al-Siddiq," meaning "the Truthful." When Prophet Muhammad (PBUH) shared the divine message, Abu Bakr did not hesitate to recognize the truth and become one of the first converts to Islam.

As the early Muslim community faced persecution in Mecca, Abu Bakr's wealth and influence were employed to secure the freedom of enslaved Muslims, demonstrating his commitment to justice and compassion. When the opposition grew fierce, and the Prophet's life was in peril, Abu Bakr selflessly offered his own life, wealth, and family in defense of the Messenger of God.

The pivotal moment in Abu Bakr's story came during the Hijra, the migration from Mecca to Medina. He accompanied Prophet Muhammad (PBUH) on this arduous journey through the unforgiving desert, facing numerous challenges with unwavering resolve. His sacrifice and loyalty during this journey solidified his place as a close confidant of the Prophet.

In Medina, Abu Bakr continued to excel in his role as a leader and advisor. When the Prophet passed away, the Muslim community faced a critical juncture, and it was Abu Bakr who emerged as the first Caliph, chosen through consensus. His leadership during this time was marked by justice, humility, and a dedication to preserving the teachings of Islam.

The story of Abu Bakr al-Siddiq is one of faith, sacrifice, and unwavering commitment to the path of righteousness. His legacy endures as an exemplar of true Islamic values, leaving an indelible mark on the pages of history. Abu Bakr's life serves as an inspiration for generations to come, reminding us all of the power of steadfastness and the beauty of unwavering faith in the face of adversity.

4. Aisha bint Abi Bakr: The Radiant Legacy

In the annals of Islamic history, few figures shine as brightly as Aisha bint Abi Bakr, the beloved wife of Prophet Muhammad (PBUH) and a luminary in her own right.

Her story is a testament to wisdom, resilience, and devotion, leaving an indelible mark on the fabric of Islam.

Aisha was born into a household of distinction, her father, Abu Bakr, being one of the closest companions of Prophet Muhammad (PBUH). From a young age, Aisha exhibited an insatiable curiosity and an unparalleled thirst for knowledge. She became known for her sharp intellect and remarkable memory, earning her a place among the foremost scholars of Islam.

Her marriage to Prophet Muhammad (PBUH) at a tender age was not just a union of hearts but a bond that would profoundly impact the course of Islamic history. Aisha was not only a devoted wife but also a confidante to the Prophet, engaging in intellectual discourse and absorbing the profound teachings of the Quran.

A pivotal moment in Aisha's life occurred during the Battle of the Camel, where she displayed extraordinary courage and leadership. Her presence on the battlefield, rallying the troops and tending to the wounded, showcased a side of Aisha that went beyond the role of a wife; she emerged as a symbol of strength and resilience.

Aisha's contribution to the preservation of Islamic knowledge is immeasurable. As one of the primary narrators of Hadith, her meticulous recollection of the sayings and actions of Prophet Muhammad (PBUH) has left an enduring legacy. Students and scholars alike flocked to learn from her, and her teachings continue to guide generations.

Despite the challenges she faced, Aisha remained a paragon of virtue, emphasizing the values of compassion, humility, and justice. Her generosity and kindness touched the lives of many, earning her respect and admiration throughout the Islamic community.

"Aisha bint Abi Bakr: The Radiant Legacy" is a story of a woman whose life exemplifies the beauty of faith, the pursuit of knowledge, and the strength that arises from unwavering commitment. Her legacy continues to inspire, reminding us that the impact of a single individual, especially one of such noble character, can resonate through time and shape the destiny of a community.

5. Umar ibn al-Khattab: The Just Caliph

In the annals of Islamic history, the story of Umar ibn al-Khattab stands as a testament to justice, leadership, and unwavering commitment to the principles of Islam.

Born into the powerful Quraysh tribe in Mecca, Umar initially opposed the growing influence of Islam. However, a transformative encounter with the words of the Quran led to his conversion, marking the beginning of a remarkable journey.

Umar's ascension to the caliphate marked a turning point in Islamic governance. Known for his strict adherence to justice, he became the second Caliph following the death of Abu Bakr. His rule was characterized by a deep sense of responsibility and fairness, earning him the title "Al-Farooq," meaning "The One Who Distinguishes Between Right and Wrong."

One of the most famous anecdotes from Umar's caliphate reflects his commitment to justice. Once, during his nightly rounds in the city, he overheard a conversation between a mother and her child. The mother, in despair, was urging her child to eat the bread she had prepared. Upon inquiry, Umar discovered that the child had not eaten for days due to the caliph's imposition of strict economic measures.

Stricken with grief, Umar immediately lifted the economic constraints, ensuring that no one in his realm would go hungry. This incident epitomizes Umar's dedication to the welfare of his people, emphasizing the importance of compassionate leadership.

Umar's justice was not limited to the elite; it extended to all, regardless of social status. There are accounts of him standing trial before his own appointed judges, ensuring that even the caliph himself was held accountable for his actions.

His governance was marked by administrative reforms, including the establishment of a welfare state, a legal code, and the introduction of a public treasury. Umar's principles of governance left an indelible mark on the foundations of Islamic administration.

However, his commitment to justice was not without personal sacrifice. Umar faced numerous threats to his life, including an assassination attempt that eventually led to his martyrdom. His death left a void in the Islamic community, but his legacy endured, shaping the principles of justice and leadership for generations to come.

The story of Umar ibn al-Khattab serves as an inspiration, a beacon of justice in the tapestry of Islamic history. It reminds us that true leadership is not defined by power alone but by the commitment to justice, compassion, and the principles of Islam.

6. Uthman ibn Affan: The Calm Navigator of Faith

Once upon a time in the early years of Islam, there lived a man of gentle demeanor and unwavering faith, known to many as Uthman ibn Affan.

His story, often overshadowed by the more tumultuous events of his time, is a testament to patience, generosity, and unyielding devotion to the principles of Islam.

Uthman was born into the powerful and respected Umayyad clan in Mecca, and his life took a transformative turn when he embraced the message of Prophet Muhammad (PBUH). His marriage to Prophet Muhammad's (PBUH) daughter, Ruqayyah, further strengthened his ties to the nascent Muslim community.

His title "Dhun-Nurain," meaning "Possessor of Two Lights," was earned not only through his marriage but also through his subsequent marriage to Umm Kulthum, another daughter of the Prophet (PBUH), after the passing of Ruqayyah. This unique honor bestowed upon Uthman reflected the Prophet's (PBUH) trust and love for this unassuming man.

However, Uthman's defining legacy emerged during his time as the third Caliph of Islam. His reign, though relatively short, was marked by significant accomplishments and challenges. One of his most notable achievements was the compilation of the Quran into a single, standardized text. This monumental task aimed to preserve the divine revelations for generations to come, ensuring the unity of the Muslim Ummah.

Uthman's commitment to social justice and compassion was evident in his efforts to provide financial aid to those in need, particularly during times of famine. His personal wealth was generously spent in the service of Islam and the welfare of its followers.

Yet, Uthman faced a turbulent period as Caliph, marred by internal strife and dissent. Despite the challenges, he maintained a steadfast demeanor, earning him the nickname "Ghani," meaning "The Generous" or "The Self-Sufficient." His detractors accused him of nepotism, but Uthman's actions were driven by a desire for unity and stability.

Tragically, the final chapters of Uthman's life unfolded in an atmosphere of turmoil. Dissent grew into rebellion, and the man who had spent his life navigating the seas of faith with calm resolve was martyred in his own home, his blood staining the Quran he had worked so diligently to preserve.

Uthman ibn Affan's story is one of sacrifice, devotion, and resilience in the face of adversity. His legacy endures as a beacon of inspiration for Muslims around the world, reminding them of the importance of unity, compassion, and the unwavering commitment to the principles of Islam. The life of Uthman serves as a profound lesson in the pages of history, encouraging believers to weather the storms of life with the calmness of a true navigator of faith.

7.Ali ibn Abi Talib: The Lion of Islam

In the heart of 7th-century Arabia, amidst the shifting sands and tribal rivalries, emerged a figure whose impact on Islam would echo through the ages—Ali ibn Abi Talib, also known as the Lion of Islam.

This is the extraordinary story of a man whose life was intertwined with the birth of a new faith, and whose unwavering commitment to justice and truth would shape the course of history.

Born into the esteemed Banu Hashim clan of the Quraysh tribe in Mecca, Ali was raised by none other than the Prophet Muhammad (PBUH) himself. From a young age, Ali displayed qualities that set him apart—courage, wisdom, and an unshakable sense of justice.

His defining moment came at the pivotal event known as the Night of the Mubahila. Chosen by the Prophet to represent the Muslim community in a spiritual contest against the Christian delegation of Najran, Ali stood firm in the face of adversity. His presence, marked by humility and conviction, left an indelible impression on all witnesses.

Ali's role in early Islamic battles showcased not only his military prowess but also his commitment to the principles of Islam. At the Battle of Badr, he distinguished himself in combat, earning the title "Asadullah" or the Lion of Allah. His leadership at the Battle of Khandaq (the Trench) demonstrated strategic brilliance and a deep sense of responsibility towards the nascent Muslim community.

As the fourth Caliph, Ali faced numerous challenges, including internal strife and external threats. His governance was marked by a tireless pursuit of justice and equality, earning him the admiration of many. However, it also led to conflicts, notably the Battle of the Camel and the Battle of Siffin, where Ali's commitment to arbitration as a means of resolving disputes demonstrated his unwavering dedication to peace.

The story of Ali ibn Abi Talib is one of sacrifice and selflessness. His profound love for Islam and his family, including his wife Fatimah and their sons Hasan and Hussain, endured through triumphs and tribulations. Ultimately, Ali's legacy is not just that of a warrior or a leader but that of a spiritual guide and a symbol of resistance against injustice.

"Ali ibn Abi Talib: The Lion of Islam" is a tale that transcends time—a narrative of a man whose life exemplifies the core values of Islam. His legacy continues to inspire generations, reminding us that true strength lies not just in physical prowess but in the unwavering commitment to righteousness and justice.

8. Fatimah bint Muhammad: The Radiant Heart of Islam

In the early days of Islam, amidst the swirling sands of Arabia, there lived a luminous soul whose presence would shape the course of history.

"Fatimah bint Muhammad: The Radiant Heart of Islam" recounts the extraordinary life of the daughter of the Prophet, a woman whose grace, strength, and unwavering devotion left an indelible mark on the nascent Muslim community.

Born to Prophet Muhammad (PBUH) and Khadijah bint Khuwaylid, Fatimah grew up in the household of love and humility. Her childhood was adorned with the wisdom of her father and the steadfastness of her mother, providing a nurturing environment that would later serve as a beacon for generations to come.

As Islam unfolded, so did the challenges faced by the Prophet and his family. Amidst the trials and tribulations, Fatimah emerged as a paragon of resilience. Her marriage to Ali ibn Abi Talib, a union marked by mutual respect and love, exemplified the sanctity of familial bonds in Islam.

The story delves into Fatimah's role as a mother, highlighting her tenderness and dedication to her children, Hasan and Hussain. The "Radiant Heart of Islam" beats with the pulse of Fatimah's unwavering faith, even in the face of adversity.

The narrative unfolds the pivotal moments in Fatimah's life, from the poignant incident of the attack on her home to her profound grief at the loss of her father, the Prophet Muhammad (PBUH). The anguish she endured during these trials serves as a testament to her strength and spiritual depth.

The tale concludes with Fatimah's serene departure from this world, leaving behind a legacy that transcends time. Her exemplary life serves as a source of inspiration, a source of light that continues to guide Muslims on the path of compassion, resilience, and unwavering faith.

"Fatimah bint Muhammad: The Radiant Heart of Islam" is not just a story; it is a journey through the annals of Islamic history, a tribute to a woman whose existence continues to resonate with the hearts of believers around the world.

9. Hamza ibn Abdul-Muttalib: The Lion of Islam

In the early days of Islam, there emerged a figure whose courage and strength would leave an indelible mark on the history of the faith.

Hamza ibn Abdul-Muttalib, the uncle of Prophet Muhammad (PBUH), earned the esteemed title "The Lion of Islam" for his unwavering commitment to justice and his fearless stance in the face of adversity.

Hamza was known for his physical prowess and hunting skills, earning him respect among the Quraysh in pre-Islamic Arabia. However, it was his conversion to Islam that would truly define his legacy. The story of Hamza's acceptance of Islam is one of profound impact.

One day, a slave named Sumayyah bint Khayyat was being brutally persecuted by her owner, Abu Jahl, for embracing Islam. Witnessing this injustice, Hamza's heart stirred with anger and compassion. Unable to tolerate the cruelty, he confronted Abu Jahl and declared his own acceptance of Islam, defying the societal norms that bound him.

This pivotal moment marked a turning point in the early Muslim community. Hamza's conversion fortified the ranks of the believers and struck fear into the hearts of those who opposed Islam. The Lion of Islam had emerged.

As the uncle of Prophet Muhammad (PBUH), Hamza played a crucial role in the early battles of Islam. His bravery on the battlefield became the stuff of legends. At the Battle of Badr, his strength and valor turned the tide, earning him a place among the ten companions guaranteed paradise by the Prophet.

Yet, amidst his fierce exterior, Hamza possessed a heart filled with kindness and loyalty. His love for the Prophet (PBUH) was unwavering, and he stood as a pillar of support during times of trial.

Tragically, Hamza met his end at the Battle of Uhud, martyred while defending the Prophet (PBUH) and the Muslim community. His sacrifice became a symbol of steadfastness and commitment to the principles of Islam.

The legacy of Hamza ibn Abdul-Muttalib lives on—a tale of a man who transitioned from the "Lion of the Desert" to the "Lion of Islam." His story inspires generations to come, teaching us that strength, courage, and justice can prevail even in the face of adversity.

10. Bilal ibn Rabah: Echoes of Faith and Freedom

In the annals of Islamic history, the story of Bilal ibn Rabah stands as an enduring testament to faith, resilience, and the pursuit of freedom.

Born into slavery in Mecca, Bilal's life took an extraordinary turn when he embraced the message of Islam preached by Prophet Muhammad (PBUH).

Bilal's journey unfolded against the backdrop of a society resistant to the revolutionary ideas of equality and monotheism. His unwavering faith and deep conviction in the message of Islam earned him both admiration and disdain. The title "Bilal ibn Rabah: Echoes of Faith and Freedom" encapsulates the profound impact of his life.

The tale begins with Bilal enduring unspeakable hardships, subjected to the brutalities of slavery. However, his heart found solace in the message of oneness of God brought by Prophet Muhammad (PBUH). His faith blossomed despite the relentless persecution he faced for embracing Islam.

The turning point arrived when Bilal, tortured and oppressed, was given the opportunity to renounce his faith and escape the torment. His response echoed through the ages, "Ahad! Ahad!" (One God! One God!), affirming his unyielding belief in the face of adversity.

Bilal's story reached its zenith during the migration to Medina, where his freedom was granted, and his value as a devout Muslim was recognized. His transformation from a persecuted slave to the first muezzin, the caller to prayer, symbolizes the emancipation of the human spirit through faith.

As the voice that echoed across the hills of Medina, Bilal's adhan became a melody of liberation, inspiring others to embrace Islam. His journey reflects the transformative power of faith, breaking the chains of oppression and ushering in an era of spiritual freedom.

The narrative unfolds with Bilal's pivotal role in key battles, his unwavering loyalty to Prophet Muhammad (PBUH), and his subsequent contributions to the nascent Muslim community. The echoes of Bilal's faith and freedom continue to resonate, reminding generations of the enduring power of belief in the face of adversity.

The story of Bilal ibn Rabah transcends time, inviting reflection on the principles of justice, equality, and the indomitable spirit that defines the essence of Islam. His legacy lives on as a beacon of inspiration, encouraging all to rise above challenges and pursue a path guided by faith and freedom.

11. Khalid ibn al-Walid: The Sword of Allah

In the annals of Islamic history, the story of Khalid ibn al-Walid stands as a testament to courage, military genius, and a transformative journey of faith.

Known as the "Sword of Allah," Khalid's life is a gripping narrative that unfolds against the backdrop of early Islam.

Born into the influential Quraysh tribe in Mecca, Khalid initially opposed the teachings of Prophet Muhammad (PBUH). However, his destiny took a dramatic turn during the Battle of Uhud when he witnessed the unwavering determination and steadfastness of the Muslim community, led by the Prophet himself.

Driven by a newfound curiosity and a thirst for truth, Khalid embarked on a quest for knowledge. His journey led him to embrace Islam, marking the beginning of a remarkable transformation. Recognizing his strategic brilliance and military prowess, Khalid was appointed by Prophet Muhammad (PBUH) as a commander in various crucial battles.

The Battle of Mu'tah showcased Khalid's exceptional leadership as he valiantly led the Muslim forces, earning the title "The Sword of Allah" for his unmatched skills on the battlefield. His strategic brilliance played a pivotal role in the victories at battles such as Yarmouk and Qadisiyyah, leading to the expansion of the Islamic empire.

Despite his military success, Khalid ibn al-Walid remained humble and devoted to the principles of justice and compassion. His legacy extends beyond the battlefield; he played a vital role in the administration and governance of the newly formed Islamic state.

The story of Khalid ibn al-Walid is a multifaceted journey—marked by personal transformation, unwavering faith, and an enduring commitment to justice. It serves as an inspiration for generations, illustrating that even those with a complex past can evolve into pillars of strength and virtue within the framework of Islam. "Khalid ibn al-Walid: The Sword of Allah" encapsulates the essence of a man whose life exemplified the principles of faith, courage, and leadership in the early Islamic era.

12. Zayd ibn Harithah: A Journey of Loyalty and Liberation

In the bustling markets of Mecca, amidst the clamor of traders and the whispers of destiny, a young boy named Zayd ibn Harithah embarked on a journey that would shape not only his own fate but also the course of Islamic history.

Born into the household of a noble Meccan, Zayd faced an uncertain childhood as an orphan. Fate, however, had grand plans for him. His charismatic presence caught the attention of a prominent figure in Mecca, none other than the beloved Prophet Muhammad (PBUH). At a time when societal norms were shifting and the call of Islam echoed through the city, Zayd found himself at the center of a remarkable tale.

The story begins with Zayd's adoption by the Prophet Muhammad (PBUH), a testament to the Prophet's commitment to justice and compassion. As the young boy became an integral part of the Prophet's household, he imbibed the values of loyalty, humility, and resilience.

Zayd's journey took a poignant turn when his biological father, Harithah, sought to reclaim him. The Prophet, exemplifying the essence of justice, gave Zayd the choice to decide his fate. In a moment that echoed through eternity, Zayd chose to remain with the man who had become not just a guardian but a beacon of light in his life.

As the pages of Zayd's story unfold, readers witness his unwavering loyalty on the battlefield. Zayd ibn Harithah emerged as a formidable warrior, standing alongside the Prophet in pivotal moments of early Islamic conquests. His bravery in the face of adversity and commitment to the principles of Islam earned him a place among the honored companions.

The narrative concludes with Zayd's ultimate sacrifice in the Battle of Mu'tah. His heroic deeds, marked by courage and selflessness, left an indelible mark on the hearts of believers. Zayd's legacy transcends time, serving as a testament to the transformative power of faith, loyalty, and the enduring bond between a man and his adopted son.

"Zayd ibn Harithah: A Journey of Loyalty and Liberation" is a tale that resonates with the essence of Islam, offering a glimpse into the life of a remarkable individual whose unwavering commitment to justice and faith echoes through the corridors of history.

13. The Wisdom Bearer - Abdullah ibn Abbas

Once upon a time, in the golden age of Islam, there lived a young man named Abdullah ibn Abbas.

His story is one of knowledge, humility, and a profound connection with the teachings of Prophet Muhammad (PBUH).

Abdullah, a cousin of the Prophet, was born into a family deeply rooted in the early Islamic community. His thirst for knowledge and wisdom set him on a remarkable journey, earning him the title "The Doctor of the Ummah."

From a tender age, Abdullah demonstrated an insatiable appetite for learning. He would sit at the feet of Prophet Muhammad (PBUH), absorbing the divine revelations with an open heart and a keen mind. The Prophet recognized Abdullah's potential and prayed for him, saying, "O Allah, make him acquire a deep understanding of the religion and instruct him in the meaning and interpretation of things."

Abdullah ibn Abbas became known for his profound understanding of the Quran and Hadith. His humility, coupled with a relentless pursuit of knowledge, led him to become one of the foremost scholars of Islam. People flocked to him from far and wide, seeking guidance and enlightenment.

One of Abdullah's most significant contributions was his role in preserving the knowledge of the Prophet's sayings. He meticulously collected and compiled the Hadith, ensuring that the teachings of Islam would be passed down through generations with authenticity.

In times of uncertainty and confusion, rulers sought Abdullah's counsel, and scholars admired his wisdom. His teachings transcended borders, and his legacy as a beacon of knowledge endures to this day.

Abdullah ibn Abbas, through his dedication to scholarship and humility, left an indelible mark on the Islamic world. His story serves as an inspiration for generations, reminding us of the transformative power of wisdom, gained not only through books but through a pure heart and a sincere quest for understanding the beauty of Islam.

14. Umm Salama: The Jewel of Patience and Wisdom

In the early days of Islam, amidst the challenges and triumphs that shaped the Muslim community, there stood a remarkable woman named Umm Salama, also known as Hind bint Abi Umayya.

Her life was a tapestry woven with threads of resilience, wisdom, and unwavering faith.

Born into the powerful tribe of Makhzumi, Umm Salama witnessed the dawn of Islam in Mecca. She was initially married to Abdullah ibn Abd al-Asad, a respected companion of the Prophet Muhammad (PBUH). Together, they embraced the call to Islam, facing persecution and hardship.

Tragedy struck Umm Salama when her husband succumbed to the brutality of the Meccan opposition. A widow with four children, she faced a daunting reality. However, her unwavering commitment to her newfound faith propelled her forward.

Umm Salama's journey took a pivotal turn when the Prophet Muhammad (PBUH) proposed to her, recognizing her strength, wisdom, and unyielding faith. Accepting this proposal meant leaving her home and embarking on a life filled with uncertainty. Yet, she embraced the opportunity to be part of a greater cause.

Her marriage to the Prophet (PBUH) was a testament to her patience and understanding. In moments of difficulty, Umm Salama displayed remarkable wisdom, offering counsel that echoed through the annals of Islamic history.

The pivotal moment in Umm Salama's life came during the Treaty of Hudaybiyyah. The Prophet (PBUH) sought to negotiate peace with the Meccans, and in a demonstration of immense sacrifice, he asked his companions to shave their heads and slaughter their sacrificial animals. Initially met with hesitation, Umm Salama's insight prevailed. She advised the Prophet (PBUH) to take the first step, and her wisdom resulted in the successful conclusion of the treaty, ultimately leading to the spread of Islam.

Umm Salama continued to be a source of guidance even after the Prophet's (PBUH) passing. Her knowledge, combined with her gentle demeanor, made her a respected figure among the early Muslims.

The story of Umm Salama is one of endurance, faith, and the transformative power of patience. Through the challenges of widowhood, migration, and the complexities of early Islamic society, she emerged as a symbol of strength and wisdom, leaving an indelible mark on the history of Islam. Her legacy teaches us that in the face of adversity, patience and unwavering faith can illuminate the path to success and enlightenment.

15. The Courageous Journey of Saad ibn Abi Waqqas

In the early years of Islam, amidst the trials and triumphs of the growing Muslim community, one figure stood out for his unwavering commitment and valor – Saad ibn Abi Waqqas.

This is the real fact story of a man whose faith and courage left an indelible mark on the history of Islam.

Saad ibn Abi Waqqas, a cousin of Prophet Muhammad (PBUH), was a key figure in the Islamic military campaigns. Born into the influential clan of Banu Zuhrah, his early life was marked by encounters with the Prophet and a gradual embrace of Islam.

Conversion to Islam:
Saad's conversion to Islam was a testament to his deep conviction. Despite facing severe opposition from his own family, he embraced the message of monotheism and became one of the earliest converts. His resilience in the face of adversity foreshadowed the unyielding spirit he would later bring to the battlefield.

Battles and Leadership:
Saad's military prowess became evident in the Battle of Badr, where his courage and strategic acumen played a pivotal role in securing a significant victory for the Muslims. His leadership continued to shine in subsequent battles, including Uhud and the Battle of the Trench.

Conquest of Persia:
Saad's most significant military achievement was the conquest of Persia. Appointed by Caliph Umar ibn al-Khattab as the commander, Saad led the Muslim forces with unparalleled determination. The Battle of al-Qadisiyyah and

the fall of Ctesiphon marked a turning point in the history of the Middle East.

Legacy of Justice:
As the governor of Kufa during the caliphate of Umar, Saad exemplified justice and equity. His governance was characterized by a commitment to upholding Islamic principles, earning him a reputation as a just and fair leader.

Lasting Contributions:
Saad ibn Abi Waqqas played a crucial role in the compilation of the Quran during the caliphate of Uthman ibn Affan. His dedication to preserving the divine message ensured the transmission of the Quran for generations to come.

Conclusion:
The life of Saad ibn Abi Waqqas is a testament to the transformative power of faith and the resilience of the human spirit. From the early days of Islam to the conquests that reshaped the map of the world, Saad's unwavering commitment to his beliefs and his exemplary leadership continue to inspire generations of Muslims. His legacy remains etched in the annals of Islamic history, a shining example of faith, courage, and dedication.

16. Abu Huraira: The Cat and the Companion

Once upon a time in the bustling city of Medina, there lived a man named Abu Huraira, whose life would become a tale of unwavering faith, compassion, and an unexpected friendship with a furry companion.

Abu Huraira, whose name means "Father of the Kitten," was a devoted companion of Prophet Muhammad (PBUH). Despite his challenging early life, Abu Huraira found solace and purpose in the teachings of Islam. His days were spent in the company of the Prophet, absorbing the wisdom that would later shape the foundations of Islamic knowledge.

One day, as Abu Huraira roamed the streets of Medina, he encountered a small, hungry kitten. His heart softened, and he decided to share the little food he had with the furry creature. This simple act of kindness marked the beginning of a unique bond between Abu Huraira and the kitten.

As Abu Huraira continued his journey with the Prophet, the kitten, now named Muezza, faithfully followed. Muezza became a beloved companion, not only to Abu Huraira but also to the entire community. People marveled at the gentleness with which Abu Huraira treated the kitten, and soon, Muezza became a symbol of compassion and mercy.

One day, as the companions gathered in the mosque, Prophet Muhammad (PBUH) noticed Muezza nestled in Abu Huraira's arms. The Prophet smiled and shared a profound lesson about mercy and kindness towards all of Allah's creations. He emphasized the value of compassion even towards the smallest creatures, for in their care, a great reward awaited.

Abu Huraira, deeply moved by the Prophet's words, continued to exemplify compassion throughout his life. His legacy extended beyond his scholarly contributions, as his story became a beacon of kindness, teaching generations the importance of empathy and care for all living beings.

As the years passed, Abu Huraira's name echoed through history, not only as a prominent companion of Prophet Muhammad (PBUH) but also as the loving guardian of Muezza, the cat who had found a forever home in the heart of a man dedicated to embodying the teachings of Islam.

And so, the story of Abu Huraira, the Cat, and the Companion became a timeless narrative of compassion, reminding believers that in the smallest acts of kindness, there lies the potential to leave an everlasting impact on the world.

17. Umm Ayman (Barakah): The Eternal Supporter

In the annals of Islamic history, there exists a remarkable woman whose life intertwined with the very fabric of the Prophet Muhammad's (PBUH) household.

Umm Ayman, affectionately known as Barakah, emerged as an enduring symbol of loyalty, care, and unwavering devotion.

Born into the servitude of Prophet Muhammad's (PBUH) noble family, Umm Ayman became an integral part of the household. Her story begins in the harsh terrain of Mecca, where she witnessed the early struggles of Islam. Barakah, though a servant, was not defined by her status; rather, she stood out for her resilience, kindness, and unyielding faith.

During the turbulent times of persecution, it was Umm Ayman who provided solace to the Prophet (PBUH) during his formative years. She was not just a caretaker; she became a motherly figure, nurturing him with a love that transcended the boundaries of blood ties.

As the fledgling Muslim community faced adversity, Umm Ayman stood steadfast. Her commitment was tested during the Migration to Medina, where she traversed the arduous journey alongside the Prophet (PBUH) and his family. Her strength and determination mirrored the essence of the early Muslim spirit.

In the oasis of Medina, Umm Ayman's role evolved. She continued to be a pillar of support, witnessing the triumphs and trials of the growing Muslim ummah. Her house became a sanctuary, a place of wisdom, and a hub for those seeking guidance.

The pages of history immortalize Umm Ayman's unique status. She bore witness to pivotal moments, including the

Battles of Badr and Uhud. Her commitment to Islam and the Prophet (PBUH) was unwavering, earning her the lasting title of "Barakah" – the blessed one.

As years passed, Umm Ayman's legacy continued to radiate. She played a pivotal role in the upbringing of Prophet Muhammad's (PBUH) beloved grandchildren, Hassan and Hussain, embodying the values of love, compassion, and wisdom.

The story of Umm Ayman (Barakah) is a testament to the profound impact one individual can have on the course of history. Her life serves as an inspiration, reminding us that true greatness lies not in titles or positions but in the sincerity of one's heart and the unwavering commitment to principles of love, loyalty, and faith.

18. Zubair ibn al-Awwam: The Unyielding Lion of Islam

Once upon a time in the early days of Islam, a noble and courageous figure emerged, leaving an indelible mark on the history of the Muslim Ummah.

His name was Zubair ibn al-Awwam, a man of unyielding determination and unwavering faith.

Zubair was born into the esteemed Banu Hashim tribe, closely related to the Prophet Muhammad (PBUH). From a young age, he exhibited qualities of bravery and loyalty that would later define his legacy. As the cousin of the Prophet and a close companion, Zubair stood alongside the Messenger of Allah through the triumphs and tribulations that marked the early years of Islam.

One of the defining moments in Zubair's life occurred during the Battle of Badr, where he showcased unparalleled courage on the battlefield. His skill with the sword and unshakable resolve earned him the title "The Lion of Badr," a testament to his prowess and dedication to the cause of Islam.

Zubair's unwavering support for the Prophet (PBUH) extended beyond the battlefield. His commitment to justice and righteousness made him a trusted advisor to the early Muslim community. His wise counsel was sought on matters of governance and interpersonal conflicts, showcasing not only his bravery in battle but also his wisdom in matters of the heart and mind.

As Islam continued to spread, Zubair remained at the forefront of pivotal moments in Islamic history. His role in the Battle of Uhud and other significant events cemented his reputation as a steadfast defender of the faith.

Yet, Zubair's legacy goes beyond his martial prowess. His humility, generosity, and dedication to the teachings of Islam endeared him to the hearts of believers. He was known for his acts of kindness, often giving away his wealth to those in need without seeking recognition or reward.

However, the pinnacle of Zubair's devotion to Islam came during the Caliphate of Umar ibn al-Khattab. Despite their familial ties, Zubair never hesitated to hold Umar accountable when he believed the caliph was deviating from the path of justice. This courageous stand, rooted in a commitment to righteousness, exemplified Zubair's integrity and his refusal to compromise on the principles of Islam.

Tragically, Zubair met his end during the tumultuous events surrounding the caliphate of Ali ibn Abi Talib. His unwavering commitment to justice led him to take a principled stand in a time of internal strife, a decision that ultimately resulted in his martyrdom.

The story of Zubair ibn al-Awwam serves as a beacon of inspiration for generations to come. His life exemplifies the true spirit of Islam — a balance of strength and compassion, justice and humility. The Lion of Islam, Zubair, continues to roar through the annals of history, reminding us that true success lies in unwavering faith and steadfast commitment to the principles of righteousness.

19. Sumayyah bint Khayyat: A Trailblazer in Faith

In the early years of Islam, during a period marked by persecution and hardship, one woman's unwavering faith and steadfastness became a beacon of inspiration for generations to come.

This is the remarkable story of Sumayyah bint Khayyat, the first martyr in Islam.

Sumayyah was born into the humble household of Yasir and his wife, Sumayyah, in the city of Mecca. The family, like many others, faced the harsh realities of societal rejection as they embraced the message of the Prophet Muhammad (PBUH). Sumayyah, along with her family, bore the brunt of relentless persecution.

As the oppression intensified, Sumayyah's faith only deepened. Her courage and commitment to the message of monotheism stood as a testament to the strength that Islam provided in the face of adversity. Sumayyah and her family faced physical and emotional torture, yet their spirits remained unbroken.

The turning point came when the tyrannical leaders of Mecca sought to crush the nascent Muslim community. Sumayyah's resilience and unyielding faith drew the attention of the Quraysh leaders, who subjected her to unspeakable torture. Despite the pain inflicted upon her, Sumayyah refused to renounce her faith.

Sumayyah's courage reached its zenith when, under the scorching Arabian sun, she became the first martyr in Islam. Her steadfastness in the face of oppression and her refusal to abandon her beliefs earned her a revered place in Islamic history.

Sumayyah bint Khayyat's story transcends time, teaching us the invaluable lesson of unwavering commitment to our principles. Her sacrifice paved the way for future generations of Muslims to practice their faith freely, reinforcing the notion that faith can be a source of strength even in the darkest moments.

The legacy of Sumayyah bint Khayyat endures as a symbol of resilience, faith, and the indomitable human spirit. Her story is a reminder that, even in the face of adversity, the pursuit of truth and justice can inspire others to stand firm in their beliefs, echoing through the ages as a beacon of light in the history of Islam.

20. Abdul-Rahman ibn Awf: A Tale of Generosity and Compassion

In the bustling markets of Mecca, amidst the clamor of merchants and the vibrant tapestry of Arabian life, lived a man whose heart shone brighter than the gold that adorned the city.

His name was Abdul-Rahman ibn Awf, a figure whose legacy would become synonymous with generosity and compassion.

Abdul-Rahman was not born into opulence; rather, he rose from humble beginnings to become one of the wealthiest and most benevolent figures of his time. His story begins with the early days of Islam when he, along with his close friend Uthman ibn Affan, embraced the teachings of Prophet Muhammad (PBUH).

As a successful merchant, Abdul-Rahman amassed wealth through honest trade, embodying the values of integrity and hard work. However, it was his unparalleled generosity that set him apart. The title "The Golden Heart of Abdul-Rahman" aptly describes his willingness to share his wealth without hesitation, earning him the nickname "The Man with Two Gardens."

The tale unfolds as Abdul-Rahman's benevolence extends beyond the realms of commerce. During the Hijra, the migration from Mecca to Medina, he selflessly offered financial assistance to those in need, solidifying his reputation as a pillar of support within the growing Muslim community. His open-handedness reached its zenith during the Battle of Tabuk when he contributed a substantial portion of his wealth to fund the expedition, ensuring the welfare of his fellow Muslims.

The story also delves into his unwavering loyalty to the Prophet Muhammad (PBUH) and the pivotal role he played in various significant events in Islamic history. His commitment to Islam and its principles continued even after the passing of the Prophet, as he played a crucial role in the election of the third Caliph, Uthman ibn Affan.

"The Golden Heart of Abdul-Rahman ibn Awf" narrates how one man's commitment to compassion and generosity not only elevated his own standing but became an enduring example for generations to come. This tale serves as a timeless reminder that true wealth lies not in gold and silver but in the kindness and benevolence that emanate from a golden heart.

21. Ammar ibn Yasir: Faith Unbroken, Trials Endured

In the early years of Islam, a remarkable figure emerged, embodying the essence of faith, perseverance, and resilience.

Ammar ibn Yasir, born into a humble family in Mecca, witnessed the dawn of Islam under the oppressive shadow of Quraysh. His story, "Faith Unbroken, Trials Endured,"

illuminates the steadfast spirit that defined the early Muslim community.

As one of the earliest converts to Islam, Ammar faced relentless persecution alongside his family. His parents, Yasir and Sumayyah, were among the first martyrs in Islamic history, their unwavering commitment to their newfound faith leaving an indelible mark on Ammar's heart.

Ammar's journey took a tragic turn during the infamous years of the Meccan persecution. Subjected to unimaginable torture and cruelty, Ammar did not waver in his devotion to Allah and the Prophet Muhammad (PBUH). In the face of adversity, he found strength in the words of the Prophet, "Endure patiently, O family of Yasir, for your destination is paradise."

The turning point came with the migration to Medina, a city of hope and refuge. Ammar's resilience and commitment caught the attention of Prophet Muhammad (PBUH), who cherished him as a close companion. Amidst the challenges of the Battle of Badr, Uhud, and the trench, Ammar fought valiantly, earning the admiration of fellow Muslims.

Yet, the true test awaited Ammar during the Battle of Siffin. Caught in the midst of a tumultuous political conflict, he found himself torn between two factions of the Muslim community. Despite the challenges and moral dilemmas, Ammar clung steadfastly to his principles, refusing to compromise his faith for political expediency.

Tragically, Ammar faced martyrdom in the Battle of Siffin, a stark reminder of the sacrifices made by those who stood firm in their convictions. His unwavering commitment to justice and truth left an enduring legacy, inspiring generations to come.

"Ammar ibn Yasir: Faith Unbroken, Trials Endured" narrates the life of a man whose journey encapsulates the early struggles of Islam. It serves as a testament to the unyielding spirit of those who embraced faith against all odds, leaving an indelible mark on the pages of Islamic history.

22. Umm Kulthum: The Radiant Sister of Umar ibn al-Khattab

In the bustling streets of Mecca during the early years of Islam, there lived a remarkable woman named Fatimah bint al-Khattab, more affectionately known as Umm Kulthum.

While history often shines its light on the prominent figures of the time, Umm Kulthum's story stands as a testament to the strength, faith, and resilience that existed in the shadows.

Umm Kulthum was the sister of Umar ibn al-Khattab, the renowned second Caliph of Islam. Though Umar was known for his strict demeanor and unwavering commitment to justice, Umm Kulthum's character radiated with kindness, compassion, and unwavering support for her brother.

As a devout Muslim, Umm Kulthum faced the challenges of a society undergoing a transformation. Her home was a refuge for those persecuted for embracing Islam. Umar, before his conversion, was one of the staunchest opponents of the new faith. Umm Kulthum's patience and prayers played a significant role in the eventual conversion of her brother.

During times of adversity, when the early Muslim community faced harsh persecution, Umm Kulthum's home became a sanctuary. She opened her doors to those who sought solace, embodying the principles of hospitality and generosity taught by Prophet Muhammad (PBUH).

Umm Kulthum's unwavering faith was not only a source of strength for her brother but also a guiding light for the entire community. Her acts of kindness and love were instrumental in fostering a sense of unity among the early Muslims.

As Islam spread and the Muslim community grew, Umm Kulthum's legacy continued to shine. Her role in supporting her brother and the community became a cornerstone of the values upheld by the early Muslims. Her story serves as a reminder that even those who work quietly behind the scenes can leave an indelible mark on the pages of history.

Umm Kulthum's life was a tapestry woven with threads of faith, compassion, and resilience. Her story is a testament to the profound impact that individuals, regardless of their visibility, can have on shaping the course of history and fostering a community built on the principles of Islam.

23. Abu Ubaidah ibn al-Jarrah: The Trustworthy Sword of Islam

In the tumultuous early years of Islam, amidst the battles that shaped the destiny of a fledgling community, one name stood out for its unwavering commitment and unparalleled trustworthiness—Abu Ubaidah ibn al-Jarrah.

Abu Ubaidah, a close companion of Prophet Muhammad (PBUH), earned the title "The Trustworthy" for his unyielding integrity and loyalty. His story begins with the early days of Islam when he, along with other companions, faced persecution in Mecca. Despite the hardships, Abu Ubaidah stood firm in his faith, never wavering in the face of adversity.

As Islam spread and the community faced formidable challenges, Abu Ubaidah emerged as a pivotal figure. His military prowess and strategic acumen played a crucial role in key battles, earning him the admiration of both allies and adversaries. Yet, it was his trustworthiness that became the stuff of legend.

The story unfolds with Abu Ubaidah's pivotal role in the conquest of Jerusalem. When the city surrendered, the Christian leaders insisted that the key to the city be handed to someone they deemed trustworthy. Unanimously, they chose Abu Ubaidah, recognizing his reputation for honesty and justice.

His leadership continued to shine during the caliphates of Abu Bakr and Umar, where he served as a trusted advisor and military commander. His humility and selflessness endeared him to the people, making him a beloved figure in the nascent Islamic state.

The climax of Abu Ubaidah's story occurs during the devastating Plague of Amwas. As the plague ravaged the Muslim army, including prominent leaders, Abu Ubaidah found himself at the forefront of the epidemic. In a selfless act of sacrifice, he gave away the only glass of water he had to a dying soldier, choosing to face death with unwavering bravery.

The narrative concludes with Abu Ubaidah's passing, leaving behind a legacy of trust, loyalty, and sacrifice. His story is not merely one of military conquests but a testament to the qualities that defined the early Muslim community—a commitment to justice, humility in leadership, and a trustworthiness that transcended the battlefield.

"Abu Ubaidah ibn al-Jarrah: The Trustworthy Sword of Islam" is a tale of honor, sacrifice, and the enduring power of unwavering principles in the face of adversity. It serves as an inspiration for generations, reminding them of the qualities that define true leadership in the path of righteousness.

24. Jabir ibn Abdullah: The Faithful Companion and Prolific Narrator

Once upon a time in the early years of Islam, there lived a man named Jabir ibn Abdullah.

His story is one of unwavering faith, steadfast loyalty, and a commitment to preserving the wisdom of Prophet Muhammad (PBUH).

Jabir was not just a companion of the Prophet; he was a witness to the transformative moments that shaped the Islamic faith. Born into a respected family, Jabir's journey with Islam began when he embraced the teachings of Prophet Muhammad (PBUH) at a young age.

As a companion, Jabir actively participated in crucial battles alongside the Prophet, demonstrating unmatched courage and loyalty. His presence on the battlefield was marked by a deep sense of duty and a commitment to upholding the principles of justice and compassion.

However, Jabir's contributions extended beyond the battlefield. He became renowned for his insatiable quest for knowledge. Jabir was not just content with witnessing events; he sought to preserve the words and actions of Prophet Muhammad (PBUH) for future generations.

Jabir ibn Abdullah's role as a narrator of Hadith (sayings and actions of the Prophet) became his lasting legacy. His memory was a treasure trove of wisdom, and people from far and wide would seek him out to hear the profound teachings of Islam directly from someone who had walked alongside the Prophet.

His humility and dedication to preserving the authentic teachings of Islam earned him the title of "The Faithful

Companion and Prolific Narrator." Jabir's narrations would go on to become vital sources of guidance for Muslims seeking to understand the nuances of their faith.

As the years passed, Jabir ibn Abdullah continued to be a beacon of knowledge and a source of inspiration for those who sought to deepen their connection with Islam. His story teaches us the importance of loyalty, courage, and the relentless pursuit of knowledge in the path of faith.

And so, the tale of Jabir ibn Abdullah echoes through the corridors of history, reminding us that the threads of Islam are woven not only through the grand battles and momentous events but also through the dedication of individuals like Jabir, who carried the light of wisdom forward for generations to come.

25. The Humble Scholar: Abdullah ibn Masud

In the bustling streets of Mecca during the early years of Islam, there lived a man whose humility and knowledge would leave an indelible mark on the history of the Muslim Ummah.

Abdullah ibn Masud, a name not as widely known as some, but a man whose story reflects the essence of a true scholar and devoted companion of Prophet Muhammad (PBUH).

Abdullah's journey into Islam was marked by an insatiable thirst for knowledge. Born into a modest family, he found himself drawn to the teachings of the Prophet Muhammad (PBUH) during the early days of the revelation. His sincerity and genuine love for learning led him to become one of the earliest converts to Islam.

The title "The Humble Scholar" reflects Abdullah's modesty, a trait that defined his character throughout his life. Despite his deep understanding of the Quran and the Sunnah, he remained unassuming, always eager to share his knowledge without seeking recognition or praise. His humility endeared him to both the Prophet (PBUH) and his fellow companions.

The story delves into Abdullah's close companionship with Prophet Muhammad (PBUH), recounting moments when he absorbed the profound wisdom emanating from the Messenger of Allah. From the hills of Mecca to the fields of Medina, Abdullah ibn Masud's unwavering dedication to learning and practicing Islam became a beacon for those around him.

As the story unfolds, readers will witness Abdullah's pivotal role in the preservation of the Quran. Tasked by the Prophet (PBUH) himself, he played a crucial part in compiling the revelations into a written form, ensuring that the words of Allah would be safeguarded for generations to come.

"The Humble Scholar: Abdullah ibn Masud" is a narrative that celebrates the virtues of simplicity, devotion, and a lifelong commitment to seeking knowledge. Through the life of this remarkable companion, readers will gain insights into the early Islamic era, discovering the profound impact that a humble scholar can have on the shaping of an enduring legacy.

26. Hassan ibn Ali: The Radiant Beacon of Peace

Once upon a time, in the early years of Islam, there lived a remarkable figure named Hassan ibn Ali.

Born to the illustrious family of Prophet Muhammad (PBUH), Hassan was destined for greatness and would become a symbol of peace and justice.

As a child, Hassan was known for his kindness and wisdom beyond his years. Growing up in the household of the Prophet (PBUH), he absorbed the teachings of Islam and embodied its values. His love for his grandfather and the message of peace and compassion he preached became the guiding lights of his life.

As he matured, Hassan became a peacemaker, resolving conflicts with his wisdom and gentle demeanor. His commitment to justice earned him the title of "The Radiant Beacon of Peace" among his contemporaries. One of the most profound chapters in his life unfolded during a critical moment in Islamic history.

In the face of political turmoil, Hassan ibn Ali took a path less traveled. Faced with the choice of potential bloodshed within the Muslim community, he made a monumental sacrifice for the greater good. In the interest of preserving unity and preventing a devastating internal conflict, Hassan entered into a peace agreement, known as the Treaty of Hasan, with his rival faction.

His decision, marked by unparalleled wisdom and selflessness, averted a potential civil war and upheld the principles of peace and unity within the Muslim ummah. Despite the challenges and criticisms he faced, Hassan stood firm in his commitment to the teachings of Islam, demonstrating that sometimes the bravest and most powerful act is to choose peace over conflict.

Hassan ibn Ali's legacy continues to shine as a beacon of inspiration for generations to come. His story teaches us the enduring power of compassion, justice, and the pursuit of peace, even in the face of adversity. The tale of Hassan ibn Ali stands as a testament to the strength found in forgiveness, understanding, and the noble pursuit of harmony within the Muslim community and beyond.

27. Hussain ibn Ali: The Martyr's Stand

In the early 7th century, amidst the shifting sands of Karbala, a profound tale unfolded—one that would resonate through the ages as a symbol of unwavering faith, sacrifice, and the pursuit of justice.

This is the real and poignant story of Hussain ibn Ali, the grandson of Prophet Muhammad (PBUH), and his stand against tyranny.

Hussain, born to Ali ibn Abi Talib and Fatimah bint Muhammad, inherited not only noble lineage but also a legacy of integrity and righteousness. As the Umayyad caliphate took a dark turn, Yazid I ascended the throne, displaying a stark departure from the principles of justice and piety that Islam espoused.

In the face of Yazid's oppressive rule, Hussain refused to pledge allegiance, recognizing the duty bestowed upon him to preserve the true essence of Islam. His stand was not a quest for power but a courageous assertion of justice, liberty, and the very soul of the Islamic faith.

The narrative unfolds with Hussain's journey to Karbala, where a small band of followers, including women and children, faced an overwhelmingly larger army. As the scorching sun bore witness, Hussain, with unparalleled bravery, refused to yield to tyranny, choosing instead to sacrifice his life for the greater good.

The Battle of Karbala on the 10th of Muharram, 61 AH (680 CE), became a testament to Hussain's unyielding spirit. Surrounded by enemies, deprived of water, and witnessing the sufferings of his family, he stood firm, upholding the values of justice and freedom until his last breath.

The story resonates not only as a historical event but as a timeless lesson, teaching humanity that even in the face of overwhelming adversity, one person's stand for righteousness can echo through the corridors of time, inspiring generations to come.

"Hussain ibn Ali: The Martyr's Stand" is a chronicle that transcends the boundaries of time, a tale that continues to kindle the flames of resilience, fortitude, and the pursuit of a just and compassionate world.

28. The Sheltering Heart: Fatimah bint Asad's Tale of Love and Resilience

Once upon a time, in the heart of Mecca, there lived a woman whose compassion echoed through the ages.

Fatimah bint Asad, the mother of Ali ibn Abi Talib, stood as a beacon of love and resilience in the early days of Islam.

In the midst of societal turbulence and the initial resistance faced by the Prophet Muhammad (PBUH) and his followers, Fatimah bint Asad emerged as a steadfast pillar of support. Her story is one of unwavering love, sacrifice, and the embodiment of the true spirit of Islam.

Born in the city of Mecca, Fatimah bint Asad belonged to the prominent Banu Hashim tribe. Widowed at a young age, she found solace in the teachings of her nephew, Muhammad (PBUH). As Islam began to take root, she embraced it with open arms, becoming one of the early converts to the faith.

Her most defining moment came when she took in an orphaned child, Ali ibn Abi Talib, the future fourth Caliph. Fatimah bint Asad's heart, already filled with compassion, expanded to encompass the young boy who would grow up to become one of the greatest figures in Islamic history.

During the years of persecution faced by the early Muslims, Fatimah bint Asad's home became a sanctuary. She shielded the Prophet's family from the harsh realities of Mecca, providing a haven of love and protection. It was under her care that Ali ibn Abi Talib developed into a man of strength, wisdom, and unwavering faith.

When the Prophet (PBUH) declared the message of Islam openly, and the hostility towards its followers intensified, Fatimah bint Asad stood resolute. She faced the trials and tribulations of those early days with a grace that left an indelible mark on the hearts of all who knew her.

Her story reached its pinnacle during the difficult years of the boycott imposed on the Prophet's family. Fatimah bint Asad, along with her family, endured hunger and hardship, yet her spirit remained unbroken. Her steadfastness became a symbol of hope for the emerging Muslim community.

As Islam triumphed and Mecca eventually embraced the message, Fatimah bint Asad witnessed the blossoming of the faith she had held dear. Her nurturing love and resilience laid the foundation for the legacy of Ali ibn Abi Talib and, in turn, the entire lineage of the Prophet Muhammad (PBUH).

The story of Fatimah bint Asad serves as a testament to the strength that love and faith can bring even in the face of adversity. Her sheltering heart and unwavering spirit continue to inspire generations, reminding us that in the darkest moments, there exists a light fueled by love and resilience.

29. From Fire to Faith: The Journey of Salman al-Farsi

Once, in the vast expanse of Persia, a man named Salman embarked on a remarkable journey that would lead him from the flickering flames of Zoroastrianism to the radiant light of Islam.

This is the real and inspiring story of Salman al-Farsi. Salman was born into a privileged family, surrounded by wealth and comfort. However, his quest for truth and spiritual fulfillment set him on a path less traveled. Drawn by an inner longing for knowledge, Salman explored various religious traditions, including Christianity and Zoroastrianism. Yet, the embers of his seeking heart continued to burn.

The pivotal moment came when Salman encountered Christian monks who spoke of a final prophet to come in Arabia. Intrigued, he set out on a journey that would change the course of his life. He witnessed the teachings of Prophet Muhammad (PBUH) and recognized the divine truth he had been searching for.

The story unfolds as Salman faced trials and tribulations for embracing Islam. From the clutches of slavery to the heart of the Islamic community, his unwavering faith and humility captured the attention of Prophet Muhammad (PBUH) himself. Salman's knowledge, humility, and dedication made him a cherished companion of the Prophet.

The narrative weaves through Salman's participation in pivotal Islamic events, from the Battle of the Trench to the conquest of Mecca. His wisdom and loyalty earned him the admiration of his fellow Muslims, and his remarkable journey symbolizes the transformative power of faith.

"From Fire to Faith: The Journey of Salman al-Farsi" is a tale of spiritual exploration, resilience, and the triumph of truth. It serves as a timeless reminder that the path to enlightenment often leads through the shadows of doubt, and those who seek sincerely may find the light they've been searching for in the most unexpected places. Salman's story stands as a testament to the inclusive nature of Islam and the profound impact one individual's journey can have on the course of history.

30. Aisha bint Talha: The Garden of Generosity

In the bustling city of Medina, amidst the golden era of Islam, lived a remarkable woman named Aisha bint Talha.

Her story, often overshadowed by more prominent figures, unveils a tapestry woven with threads of generosity, kindness, and an unwavering commitment to virtue.

Aisha, a woman of noble lineage, earned her place in history not through political power or battlefield heroics, but through the garden of generosity she cultivated in the hearts of those around her. Her home was a haven where the fragrance of compassion lingered in the air, inviting all who entered to experience the warmth of true hospitality.

Known for her exceptional generosity, Aisha bint Talha opened her doors wide to guests, strangers, and the less fortunate. Her kindness knew no bounds, and her guests were treated not as visitors but as cherished members of an extended family. The aroma of delicious food wafted through her home, and the laughter of those gathered around her table echoed the spirit of unity and love that she fostered.

Aisha's generosity extended beyond material offerings; she possessed an innate ability to uplift the spirits of those in need. In times of difficulty, her comforting words and compassionate demeanor served as a balm to wounded souls. Her garden of generosity was not just a physical space but a sanctuary where people found solace and felt the genuine embrace of community.

Despite facing challenges and trials, Aisha bint Talha stood as a beacon of strength and resilience. Her unwavering commitment to virtuous living left an indelible mark on the hearts of those who were fortunate enough to cross her path. She lived a life that exemplified the teachings of Islam, embodying the values of compassion, kindness, and selflessness.

In the annals of Islamic history, Aisha bint Talha's story may be a modest entry, but it is a testament to the profound impact that simple acts of generosity can have on the world. Her legacy serves as an inspiration, reminding us that true wealth lies not in material possessions but in the richness of a generous heart.

"Aisha bint Talha: The Garden of Generosity" is a tale of a woman whose life blossomed with the flowers of compassion, leaving behind a fragrant legacy that continues to inspire generations to cultivate their own gardens of generosity.

www.ingramcontent.com/pod-product-compliance
Lightning Source LLC
Chambersburg PA
CBHW081154130726
47996CB00009B/3114